Guacamole Cookbook

Best Guacamole Recipe eBook With Variety of Flavors

By

Martha Stephenson

Copyright 2017 Martha Stephenson

License Notes

No part of this Book can be reproduced in any form or by any means including print, electronic, scanning or photocopying unless prior permission is granted by the author.

All ideas, suggestions and guidelines mentioned here are written for informative purposes. While the author has taken every possible step to ensure accuracy, all readers are advised to follow information at their own risk. The author cannot be held responsible for personal and/or commercial damages in case of misinterpreting and misunderstanding any part of this Book

Table of Contents

Introduction 5

Chapter 1 – Variety of Guacamole Recipes 7

    Jalapeno Pepper Guacamole Recipe 9

    Amazing Guacamole Mix 11

    Lime Juice Guacamole Recipe 13

    Various Juices Guacamole Mix 15

    Cilantro Mix Guacamole Recipe 17

    Mayonnaise Guacamole Recipe 19

Chapter 2 – Quick Mix Recipes of Guacamole 21

    Red Pepper Flakes Mix 23

    Bacon Guacamole Mix Recipe 25

    Delicious Mix of Guacamole 27

    Light and Different Guacamole 29

    Onion Mix Guacamole 31

    Egg Mixed Guacamole Recipe 33

Chapter 3 – Favorite and Top Guacamole Recipes 35

    Quick Guacamole Mix Recipe 37

    Shiso Leaves Guacamole 39

    Diced Guacamole Recipe 41

    Simple Guacamole Recipe 43

    Cayenne Guacamole Mix 45

    Mango Mix Guacamole 47

    Serrano Chile Guacamole 49

Chapter 4 – Sauces Mix Guacamole Recipes 51

    Worcestershire Sauce Guacamole Recipe 53

    Asparagus Salsa Guacamole 55

    Greek Style Yogurt Recipe 57

    Black Bean Guacamole Recipe 59

    Hot Pepper Sauce Recipe 61

    Edamame Mix Guacamole Recipe 63

Conclusion 65

About the Author 67

Author's Afterthoughts 69

Introduction

A lot of people have started to depend on the fast food because they do not have time to cook. Health has become a concern for every person nowadays because you hardly find something which is organic and good for your body. But taking out 30 minutes of your life will save you from a lot of diseases and problems which may occur in your body because of consuming fast food.

You have fast food once in a while, but it is always better to cook yourself at home which is why here is the awesome Guacamole Recipe eBook which provides you different ingredients in each recipe to try. The recipes do not take more than 20 minutes for you make and save it for later as well. You do not have to consume the recipe in one go, but you can eat it little and save it for a week!

Guacamole cookbook brings you a good life and also makes you an expert in cooking. Do not depend on fast foods because they will eventually make you weaker internally without you knowing about it. Healthy food leads to good moods as well as you will be sure that when you have cooked it, it would be accordingly to your style. There are a lot of health benefits which come along with guacamole recipes so do not just think that it is the matter of food, but it is the matter of your health. The recipes which are made of avocados keep your blood pressure normal and neutral, so you can lead a healthy lifestyle.

When you start cooking these awesome recipes, you will be able to see a dynamic change in your lifestyle which you will love for sure! All the recipes have the main ingredient which is the Avocados. The avocados make the guacamole a perfect and complete recipe so make sure not to miss on the main ingredient!

Chapter 1 – Variety of Guacamole Recipes

Avocado is a unique fruit and people do not think that you can make so many recipes out of it. It consists of carbohydrates, and you can avoid fat from it as well. It has numerous positive effects on health which are beneficial for human body. The main ingredient of guacamole recipes is avocado, which is completely nutritious. It is known as the full fruit. You can make all sorts of dishes out of avocados. It is one of the popular fruit in many countries which people love to have. There are different shapes of avocados weight different pounds so whichever one you like, you can get it easily.

Here are some of the amazing variety of Guacamole recipes which you can make and try at home with your family. There is less risk of anyone getting ill in your family if you have avocados once a week. Your immune system gets so strong that you do not fall ill easily even if there are bacteria around you. Your body fights with them to keep you safe and healthy. They will love it for sure, and it will make you lead a healthy life with providing all the necessary nutrients which your family would need throughout the week!

Jalapeno Pepper Guacamole Recipe

Cooking time: 20 minutes

Servings: 2 to 3 servings

Want a little spice in the recipe? Then do not miss out on this one!

Ingredients:

- Avocados (peeled) – 4
- Lime juice – 2 tbsp.
- Lemon juice – 2 tbsp.
- Tomatoes (diced) – 2 cans
- Red onion (diced) – ½ cup
- Jalapeno pepper (minced) – 1 large
- Garlic (minced) – 3 cloves
- Salt and pepper to taste

Cooking Instructions:

Get the bowl and add the avocado in it. Now grab the masher and mash the avocados until it reaches the paste form.

Add lime juice and lemon juice in it and mix it well. Now mix the tomatoes along with jalapeno peppers in it. Stir it well with adding red onions with garlic and salt and pepper. When ready, serve and enjoy!

Amazing Guacamole Mix

Cooking time: 9 minutes

Servings: 2 to 3 servings

One of the quick and amazing guacamole recipe which you want to have every day.

Ingredients:

- Avocados – 2
- Small onion (chopped) – 1
- Garlic (minced) – 1 clove
- Tomato (diced) – 1
- Lime juice – 1 tbsp.
- Salt and pepper to taste
- Cayenne powder – 1 tbsp.

Cooking Instructions:

Mash the avocados in a bowl and then add garlic, onion, lime juice, tomato with salt and pepper.

Mix it well with adding cayenne powder at the end. When ready, serve with your favorite meal!

Lime Juice Guacamole Recipe

Cooking time: 10 minutes

Servings: 2 to 3 servings

Adding lime juice to guacamole recipe will make it amazing for you!

Ingredients:

- Avocados (diced) – 2
- Salt to taste
- Tomato (diced) – 1
- Onion (diced) – 1
- Jalapeno peppers (chopped) – 2
- Cilantro (chopped) – ½ tbsp.
- Lime juice – 2 tbsp.

Cooking Instructions:

Get a bowl and mash the avocados properly with a fork. Then add the salt as desired. Mix well.

When done, add tomato, jalapeno peppers, onion, cilantro and lime juice in it. Combine all the ingredients with stirring well.

When done, it is ready to serve and enjoy!

Various Juices Guacamole Mix

Cooking time: 10 minutes

Servings: 2 to 3 servings

The Different flavor of juices in this recipe will make you have it again and again!

Ingredients:

- Avocados (mashed) – 2
- Lime juice – ½ tbsp.
- Orange juice – ½ tbsp.
- Pineapple juice – ½ tbsp.
- Ground cumin – 1 tsp.
- Chopped Cilantro – ¼ tbsp.
- Salt and pepper to taste

Cooking Instructions:

Grab a bowl and add avocados with lime juice, pineapple juice, orange juice, ground cumin and salt and pepper.

Mix all the ingredients well until it turns into a thick paste. Now add cilantro in it and serve when ready!

Cilantro Mix Guacamole Recipe

Cooking time: 10 minutes

Servings: 2 to 3 servings

You will surely love the taste of cilantro in this recipe and will be trying it repeatedly!

Ingredients:

- Avocados (mashed) – 5
- Lemon juice – 2 tbsp.
- Green onion (minced) – ½ cup
- Cilantro (chopped) – ½ cup
- Salt and pepper to taste

Cooking Instructions:

Get a bowl and add the avocados mash in it with adding lemon juice. Now add the green onions and mix well.

When done, spread the cilantro all over the paste and sprinkle salt and pepper to taste. When done, it is ready to serve!

Mayonnaise Guacamole Recipe

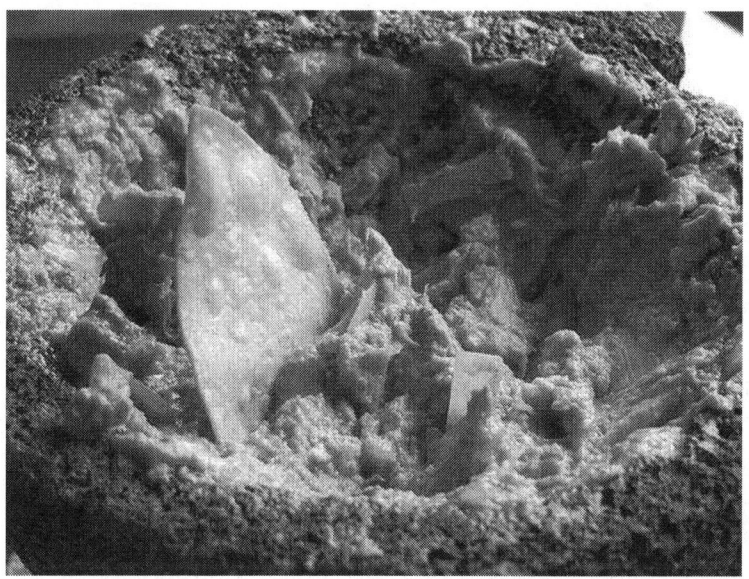

Cooking time: 10 minutes

Servings: 2 to 3 servings

Mayonnaise adds up flavor to any food but how about you try it with guacamole recipe?

Ingredients:

- Avocados (chopped) – 2
- Salsa – 2 tbsp.
- Mayonnaise – 2 tbsp.
- Chili powder – ¼ tsp.
- Salt and pepper to taste

Cooking Instructions:

Grab a bowl and add avocados with mayonnaise, salsa, salt and pepper with chili powder. Mix well.

If you wish to have it cold, then keep in it the fridge for a while and then serve otherwise it can be consumed right away after is ready!

Chapter 2 – Quick Mix Recipes of Guacamole

Guacamole recipes contain potassium higher than a banana. Nowadays, people are not consuming much of potassium food due to which they are facing diseases in their life. You do not get to know that you are missing on a specific nutrient due to which it can be affecting your health. You will be exposed to different diseases without any fault, but that would be because of consuming the wrong food. You need to eat healthily and the foods which provide you necessary nutrients to lead a healthy lifestyle. Potassium helps your body cell to function properly and keeps you energetic all day long.

Avocados are high in potassium and are typically known to be above banana as well. It reduces the risk of heart attacks, kidney failure, blood pressure and strokes. It is an important mineral which your body needs to keep the blood flow normal in the body. Here are some of the recipes which are made of avocado, and you should surely try them every day. They are simple and easy to make without any extra effort but to keep yourself healthy you can take out 10 minutes of your life for sure!

Red Pepper Flakes Mix

Cooking time: 10 minutes

Servings: 2 to 3 servings

Tomatillos and tomatoes mix recipe will be your favorite after you try this one!

Ingredients:

- Avocados (peeled) – 3
- Tomatillos (chopped) – 3
- Red onion (chopped) – 1
- Tomatoes (chopped) – 2
- Lime juice – 1 tbsp.
- Red pepper flakes – 1 tbsp.
- Hot pepper sauce – 2 drops
- Salt and pepper to taste

Cooking Instructions:

Get a bowl and mix tomatillos, tomatoes, red onion, avocados and lime juice in it. Mix well.

Now season the mixture with hot pepper sauce, red pepper flakes and salt and pepper as desired. Cover it and keep in refrigerator until it cools.

When ready, serve and enjoy!

Bacon Guacamole Mix Recipe

Cooking time: 15 minutes

Servings: 2 to 3 servings

If you love bacon then you will surely want to try this recipe!

Ingredients:

- Avocados – 4
- Bacon (crumbled) – 4 slices
- Tomato (chopped) – 1
- Onion (chopped) – 1
- Garlic (minced) – 1
- Salt and pepper to taste
- Hot pepper to taste

Cooking Instructions:

Get a bowl and add avocados in it with mashing it with the fork. Now add onion, tomatoes, crumbled bacon with garlic in it. Blend it well.

Mix hot pepper with salt and pepper as desired. When done, serve immediately and enjoy the delicious recipe!

Delicious Mix of Guacamole

Cooking time: 10 minutes

Servings: 2 to 3 servings

The mixture of the ingredients in this recipe will leave you mesmerized to try it again and again!

Ingredients:

- Avocados – 2
- Tomatoes – 2
- Onion (chopped) – 2
- Garlic (minced) – 2 cloves
- Lime juice – ½ tsp.
- Salt and pepper to taste

Cooking Instructions:

Add the avocados into the bowl keeping it lightly mashed with leaving some of the pieces in chunks. Now add tomatoes, garlic, lime juice, onion with salt and pepper in it.

Mix well and when ready, serve immediately.

Light and Different Guacamole

Cooking time: 11 minutes

Servings: 2 to 3 servings

You will feel light and amazing after the taste of this recipe!

Ingredients:

- Avocados – 3
- Tomatoes (diced) – 2
- Onion (minced) – 2 tbsp.
- Lemon juice – 1 tbsp.

Cooking Instructions:

Mash the avocados in a bowl with adding onion, tomatoes and lemon juice in it.

Keep it in the refrigerator for it to cool down. When ready, serve the delicious and simple recipe for guacamole with any dish.

Onion Mix Guacamole

Cooking time: 10 minutes

Servings: 2 to 3 servings

Onion make any meal delicious but how about you try it in guacamole recipes?

Ingredients:

- Avocados – 2
- Lime juice – 1 tbsp.
- Jalapeno pepper (diced) – 1
- Garlic (minced) – 2 cloves
- Onion (minced) – ½
- Tomato (diced) – 1
- Cilantro (chopped) – 1 tbsp.
- Salt and pepper to taste

Cooking Instructions:

Get a bowl and add the avocados in it with mashing it properly with a form or masher. Add the lime juice in it by mixing well.

Now mix the jalapeno pepper, onion, garlic, cilantro, tomato with salt and pepper. Combine the mixture properly and enjoy eating when done.

Egg Mixed Guacamole Recipe

Cooking time: 14 minutes

Servings: 2 to 3 servings

Love eggs? Then try this guacamole recipe mixed with eggs in it!

Ingredients:

- Eggs – 2
- Avocados – 2
- Onion (diced) – 1
- Tomato (diced) – 1
- Lime juice – 2 tbsp.
- Hot pepper sauce – 1 tsp.
- Worcestershire sauce – ½ tsp.
- Salt and pepper to taste
- Wasabi powder – 1 tsp.
- Green onion (chopped) – 1
- Cilantro (chopped) – a bunch

Cooking Instructions:

Get a pot and boil the eggs in it. When done, take it out and let it cool down. Now peel off the egg shells and then mash the eggs in a bowl.

On the other hand, mash the avocados in another bowl with adding lime juice, pepper sauce, tomato, onion, green onion, salt and pepper and wasabi powder in it. Mix it well.

Add the mashed eggs into the avocados bowl and stir it gently. When done, garnish it with cilantro, and it is ready to serve!

Chapter 3 – Favorite and Top Guacamole Recipes

One of the main nutrients which you will be able to find in avocado is fiber. It helps you to lose weight and reduce blood sugar as well. You can lower the risk of catching many diseases if you tend to consume avocados in any shape whether you add it to the salad or have a dip made out of it. There are different ways to have avocados, and you are open to whichever way you love to eat. If you love to cook it with another recipe, then you can, or if you wish to boil it simply and eat it, then you can do that also. In every way, it will provide you the necessary nutrients which your body requires on a daily basis.

It provides the soluble fiber which is known to fight the bacteria in your body. You do not tend to fall ill if you can fight the bacteria and your immune system gets strong as well. Our body tend to function at an optimal level when you consume avocados. The daily amount which you should have is about 27% which can keep you healthy all the way long. You can easily lower the level of cholesterol in your body if you consume avocados. Heart diseases are common nowadays and if you wish to stay away from consuming numerous pills then try this fruit in any way you like such as in the form of guacamole recipe or raw form. It can control the human trials, and you can live longer with it as well. Make sure to try these recipes if someone in your family is facing the issue of cholesterol!

Quick Guacamole Mix Recipe

Cooking time: 10 minutes

Servings: 2 to 3 servings

Very fewer ingredients and quick recipe to make if you do not want to stay in kitchen longer!

Ingredients:

- Avocados – 4
- Onion (minced) – 1
- Lemon juice – 1 tbsp.
- Hot pepper sauce – 2 drops
- Tomatoes (diced) – 1
- Salt and pepper to taste

Cooking Instructions:

Get a bowl and mash the avocados in it. Make sure the texture is smooth.

Now add tomatoes and onion in the mashed avocado. Mix well.

Add hot pepper sauce along with lemon juice with sprinkling salt and pepper on the top. Stir all the mixture together and serve when done!

Shiso Leaves Guacamole

Cooking time: 10 minutes

Servings: 2 to 3 servings

Try the shiso leaves recipe, and you would not be able to get over it!

Ingredients:

- Avocados – 2
- Lime juice – 1 tbsp.
- Onion (minced) – 1
- Jalapeno peppers (minced) – 2
- Shiso leaves (chopped) – 10
- Ginger root (minced) – 1 tbsp.
- Wasabi paste – 1 tsp.
- White pepper – ½ tbsp.
- Hot pepper sauce – 2 drops
- Tomato (chopped) – 1
- Salt and pepper to taste

Cooking Instructions:

Get a bowl and add lime juice, avocados, onion, shiso leaves, jalapeno pepper, white pepper, ginger, wasabi paste and hot sauce in it. Now get a mashed and mash all the ingredients. It should turn into thick paste when you are done.

Chop the tomatoes over the paste and gently mix. Add salt and pepper to taste and enjoy the delicious recipe!

Diced Guacamole Recipe

Cooking time: 10 minutes

Servings: 2 to 3 servings

An amazing start of the day with this delicious diced avocado mix!

Ingredients:

- Red onion (chopped) – ½ cup
- Cilantro (chopped) – 1 bunch
- Jalapeno (minced) – 1
- Lime juice – 1 tbsp.
- Garlic (minced) – 2 cloves
- Tomatoes (diced) – 4
- Avocados (cubed) – 4

Cooking Instructions:

Get a bowl and mix cilantro, lime juice, garlic, onion and jalapeno in it. Mix well.

Add tomatoes in it with adding avocados. Stir it gently and keep it in the refrigerator to settle before eating. When ready, serve and enjoy!

Simple Guacamole Recipe

Cooking time: 10 minutes

Servings: 2 to 3 servings

This is simple to try and you can eat it with any meal you want!

Ingredients:

- Serrano Chili – 2
- Cilantro (chopped) – ½ cup
- Onion (diced) – ¼ cup
- Salt to taste
- Avocados – 2
- Tomatoes – 1 cup
- Lime juice – 1 tbsp.

Cooking Instructions:

Chop the peppers, cilantro, and onions properly of one shape. Add them to the bowl and sprinkle salt on it. Now mash the mixture and mix it well.

Cut the avocados and scoop out the flesh of it by adding to the mixture bowl. Add lime juice in it along with tomatoes which should be mashed as well. Stir all the paste well, and when done, it is ready to serve!

Cayenne Guacamole Mix

Cooking time: 10 minutes

Servings: 2 to 3 servings

The Different flavor of cayenne powder will make you try this recipe again and again.

Ingredients:

- Chile peppers – 4
- Tomatoes – 3
- Onion – 1
- Garlic (peeled) – 2 cloves
- Olive oil – 1 tbsp.
- Avocados – 4
- Lemon juice – ½ tbsp.

- Salt and pepper to taste
- Cayenne powder – ½ tbsp.
- Cilantro (chopped) – 1/3 cup

Cooking Instructions:

Heat the oven to 350 F and prepare the baking tray.

Get a bowl and add green Chile in it with along with onion, garlic, onion, and tomatoes. Mix it well.

Spread the oil lightly on the baking tray and add the ingredients in the bowl to bake for about 10 minutes. Now take out the garlic cloves from the bowl and keep them aside.

Get a food processor and add tomatoes and garlic cloves in it. Pulse it until it turns into a thick paste. Mash the avocados on the other hand and add the tomato paste in it. Add baked mixture, lemon juice, cayenne powder and salt in it along with pepper as desired. Mix it well and then sprinkle the cilantro on it.

Serve when ready and enjoy the guacamole with chips or your favorite meal.

Mango Mix Guacamole

Cooking time: 10 minutes

Servings: 2 to 3 servings

Mango mix guacamole is all you need to have a fruity taste in your food!

Ingredients:

- Avocados – 2 ripe
- Mango (diced) – 1
- Garlic (minced) – 1 clove
- Lime juice – 2 tsp.
- Chipotle pepper – ¼ tsp.
- Salt to taste

Cooking Instructions:

Mash the avocados in a bowl until it has a smooth consistency.

Add garlic, lime juice, chipotle pepper and salt in it. Mix well.

Now gently add the diced mango and stir it lightly. When done, serve and enjoy the delicious recipe!

Serrano Chile Guacamole

Cooking time: 20 minutes

Servings: 2 to 3 servings

You will love the flavor of this recipe with avocados mixed in it.

Ingredients:

- Avocados (mashed) – 5
- Tomatoes (diced) – 3
- Serrano Chile (diced) – 1
- Garlic (chopped) – 3 cloves
- Cilantro (chopped) – ½ cup
- Lime juice – 1 tbsp.
- Olive oil – 2 tbsp.
- Salt to taste

Cooking Instructions:

Mash some of the avocados and cut half of them into small pieces. Now add tomatoes, Serrano Chile, garlic, cilantro and lime juice in it.

Mix it well with adding olive oil as well. When done, sprinkle the salt, and your favorite simple guacamole recipe is ready!

Chapter 4 – Sauces Mix Guacamole Recipes

If you are someone who is looking forward to losing weight, then you can try these guacamole recipes, and you will surely lose a lot of weight. Do not think that the sauces will increase any bit of the weight they are just there to add flavor to the food. We tend to miss out a lot when we are on a diet which is why the flavors of sauces help us retain the taste buds on our tongue, so we do not starve ourselves. The nutrients should be absorbed into our body whatever we eat so we have to make sure to consume the food which is healthy and beneficial for us.

Some of the nutrients can be fat soluble which can be combined to become fat in our body so make sure to consume the food which is less in fat soluble. Avocados are one of the fruits absorbs the nutrients and give energy to your body with not having an effect on your weight at all. You can add avocados into salad or food, but if you make the dip out of it, then you can enjoy it with any food as a side dish with having all the nutritional benefits from it as well. It has natural ingredients as well as delicious sauces which you can try. Check out the delicious recipes below to find out more about guacamole recipes which you will surely love!

Worcestershire Sauce Guacamole Recipe

Cooking time: 10 minutes

Servings: 2 to 3 servings

If you cannot have food without sauces then try this recipe to enjoy guacamole dip!

Ingredients:

- Avocado (diced) – 1
- Tomato (diced) – 1
- Red onion (diced) – ½
- Chile pepper (minced) – 1
- Salt and pepper to taste
- Garlic powder – ½ tsp.
- Worcestershire sauce – 1 tsp.
- Hot sauce – 2 drops
- Cilantro (minced) – a bunch
- Lime juice – 1 tbsp.

Cooking Instructions:

Get a bowl and add tomato, avocado, Chile pepper, salt and pepper, onion and garlic powder in it along with cilantro leaves. Mix it well.

Add lime juice and Worcestershire sauce with hot sauce in it. Stir all the ingredients and keep it in the refrigerator for half an hour. When cooled, take it out and enjoy with adding it to the tortilla chips or any of your favorite side meal with it.

Asparagus Salsa Guacamole

Cooking time: 20 minutes

Servings: 2 to 3 servings

The delicious mixture of asparagus and salsa will make you love this recipe!

Ingredients:

- Asparagus (chopped) – 24 spears
- Salsa – ½ cup
- Cilantro (chopped) – 1 tbsp.
- Garlic (minced) – 2 cloves
- Green onion (sliced) – 4
- Avocado (mashed) – 1

Cooking Instructions:

Boil the asparagus and mashed it properly when done. Mash avocado in the other bowl and then add to the asparagus paste.

Now add salsa, green onion, garlic and cilantro in it. Mix it well and serve with your favorite dressing. You can also serve it with chips around it or corn chips whichever you like.

Greek Style Yogurt Recipe

Cooking time: 14 minutes

Servings: 2 to 3 servings

You will surely love the taste of asparagus with yogurt so do not miss out on this recipe!

Ingredients:

- Asparagus – 1 ½ pounds
- Green style yogurt – 1 tbsp.
- Lime juice – 1 tbsp.
- Fresh cilantro – 1 tbsp.
- Green onions (sliced) – 2
- Jalapeno pepper (minced) – ½
- Garlic (minced) – 1 tbsp.
- Tomato (diced) – 1
- Worcestershire sauce – ½ tsp.
- Hot pepper sauce – 1 dash
- Salt and pepper to taste

Cooking Instructions:

Steam the asparagus in the steamer for about 4 minutes. When done, add it to the food processor and pulse it for 2 minutes until mashed.

Add yogurt, cilantro, lime juice, jalapeno pepper, green onions, Worcestershire sauce, tomato, garlic and hot pepper sauce in a large bowl. Gently mix it and add the asparagus paste. Mix well.

When ready, sprinkle salt and pepper as desired and serve to enjoy!

Black Bean Guacamole Recipe

Cooking time: 12 minutes

Servings: 2 to 3 servings

The cheese mixed guacamole recipe with black beans is all you need to have fun food.

Ingredients:

- Avocado (mashed) – 1
- Black beans – 1 can
- Lime juice – 1 tbsp.
- Garlic (minced) – 2 cloves
- Cheddar cheese (shredded) – 1/3 cup
- Sea salt to taste

Cooking Instructions:

Get a microwave bowl and mix the avocado with black beans. If you wish to mash the black beans you can do that or you can just simply add it to the mashed avocado.

Now add lime juice and garlic in it with mixing well along with sea salt. Stir it well.

Sprinkle the cheddar cheese on the top, so it covers the mixture. Microwave it for 2 minutes and serve when ready.

Hot Pepper Sauce Recipe

Cooking time: 15 minutes

Servings: 2 to 3 servings

Want to have hot pepper flavor in the recipe? Then this one is for you!

Ingredients:

- Avocados (peeled) – 4
- Onion (diced) – 1
- Tomatoes (diced) – 1
- Lemon juice – 1
- Hot pepper sauce – 5 dashes
- Salt to taste

Cooking Instructions:

Grab a bowl and mash the avocados in it. Make sure it turns into a smooth paste.

Now add pepper sauce, salt, and lemon juice. Mix it well with the spoon and serve to enjoy!

Edamame Mix Guacamole Recipe

Cooking time: 15 minutes

Servings: 2 to 3 servings

If you love the flavor of edamame then this is the recipe for you to try now!

Ingredients:

- Shelled Edamame – 6 oz.
- Onion (chopped) – ½
- Cilantro (chopped) – 1 bunch
- Olive oil – 2 tbsp.
- Avocado (cubed) – 1 large
- Lemon juiced – 1
- Garlic sauce – 1 tbsp.
- Salt and pepper to taste

Cooking Instructions:

Get a food processor and add edamame, cilantro, onion and olive oil in it. Make sure it gets chopped finely.

Add lemon juice, avocado and garlic sauce in it by mixing it well. Now pulse it again with adding salt and pepper.

When done, pour it into the bowl and keep it in the refrigerator for a while before eating.

Conclusion

We all know that avocados are healthy for our living. They provide us all the nutrients which we need to survive with full energy and keeps us motivated. People do not like to have the hard and raw avocados due to which they forward to some recipes which can be made out of them. The recipes which are made out of avocados are called guacamole recipes. This eBook gives you a great insight on all the possible recipes of guacamole. Each recipe has avocado in it with different other ingredients which change the taste of the recipe for you.

You just need to know the right technique to make it, and you will have an amazing recipe right in front of you. Instead of buying different salsa from the stores, you can make your dip at home to try with any food you want. People love to have fried food, and the guacamole recipes can set best with them to add flavor to it more. Guacamole recipes are delicious, and it is the best dip which you can make at home.

You will be able to find different recipes from everywhere, but these are special ones which can be made at home and without any effort in it. They take less than half an hour to be made and that too with hygiene. You know all the necessary ingredients and know that it will be healthy for you to consume the dip. There is no chili flavor involved in the recipes, so they are pretty normal to eat and consume with any food. Anyone can eat it whether it is a child or someone adult because it is the best fruit to provide you numerous nutrients.

The amazing 25 recipes give you the option to make a new one every day and not get tired of it. All the recipes are quick and easy to make with amazing ingredients which you will be able to find at home. You do not have to step out especially to find the ingredients because they are commonly used in every kitchen. Make the recipes and enjoy with your friends and family to have a great time over the weekend. They will love it when you make the new recipe every day.

About the Author

Martha is a chef and a cookbook author. She has had a love of all things culinary since she was old enough to help in the kitchen, and hasn't wanted to leave the kitchen since. She was born and raised in Illinois, and grew up on a farm, where she acquired her love for fresh, delicious foods. She learned many of her culinary abilities from her mother; most importantly, the need to cook with fresh, homegrown ingredients if at all possible, and how to create an amazing recipe that everyone wants. This gave her the perfect way to share her skill with the world; writing cookbooks to spread the message that fresh, healthy food really can, and does, taste delicious. Now that she is a mother, it is more important than ever to make sure that healthy food is available to the next generation. She hopes to become a household name in cookbooks for her delicious recipes, and healthy outlook.

Martha is now living in California with her high school sweetheart, and now husband, John, as well as their infant daughter Isabel, and two dogs; Daisy and Sandy. She is a stay at home mom, who is very much looking forward to expanding their family in the next few years to give their daughter some siblings. She enjoys cooking with, and for, her family and friends, and is waiting impatiently for the day she can start cooking with her daughter.

Author's Afterthoughts

Thanks ever so much to each of my cherished readers for investing the time to read this book!

I know you could have picked from many other books but you chose this one. So a big thanks for downloading this book and reading all the way to the end.

If you enjoyed this book or received value from it, I'd like to ask you for a favor. Please take a few minutes to post an honest and heartfelt review on *Amazon.com*. Your support does make a difference and helps to benefit other people.

Thanks!

Martha Stephenson

Made in the USA
Lexington, KY
24 March 2018